Introduction

Welcome to fire up. Assuming that this is your first effort to begin another endeavor, I might want to wish you all the accomplishment with your new business. Most organizations come up short in their first year. The primary driver of disappointment isn't outer real factors like monetary slump yet rather an absence of monetary control and poor key administration, two factors that are tended to in this book. Presently recollect, making a buck's difficult. It's not easy to start your own business and make a million dollars and if it was, everybody would be a millionaire. It takes genuine coarseness, enthusiasm, constancy, responsibility, information and talent.

Do you adapt well under tension? Is it truc that you are OK with consistent change? How would you respond to disappointment? Do you manage struggle well? Are you prepared to hustle?

Starting up your own business is an all-consuming goliath that will assume control over your life, for at minimum the principal little while at any rate. It will negatively affect you, your family, your very own abundance, your side interests and basically whatever else you have in your life. You will work extended periods of time, manage a greater number of issues in daily than you would typically manage in a week and in the event that you can't hustle, quit while you're ahead.

I was as of late asked by a partner what it resembled maintaining my own new company, up until that point I hadn't given it any thought. In the primary year, I felt like I was in some sort of Battle Creek fight with things coming at me from all sides. A steady and consistently changing business attack that extended me to the limit.

They say you don't know what you're made of until you're tested. First year of start-up is going to show you what you are made of. Running a Start-up business separates the boys from the men, the women from the girls. Just when you think you have taken as much as you think you can take, guess what? Tomorrow there will be more!

Whether you succeed or fall flat with your new pursuit, it is critical to be benevolent to yourself as you work eagerly towards accomplishing your objectives. Get some down time for you and adapt to any and all challenges. Keep in mind, just the solid survive.

There are not many things in this world as fulfilling as making a business you began a triumph. It is a brilliant inclination when you see something you made from nothing being delighted in by individuals and bringing in cash. It is an awesome inclination to see workers sharing your vision and trusting in your brand.

When I was running my first organization, each night when I left the workplace I would continuously stop out the front of the workplace and gaze toward the sign. I was unable to be any prouder, there it was, and my business had turned into a reality. Workers were getting by from a thought I had, clients were partaking in the items and administrations being presented by my business.

I hadn't the faintest idea what I was doing when I began my first business. I in a real sense white knuckled it during each time of activity. I caused problems as I went ahead day on day without a solitary sign what I was truly doing. The organization was moderately fruitful and I claimed and worked it for quite some time, and consistently I discovered some new information! One thing is without a doubt however, assuming I had begun that organization currently knowing what I know now, it would have turned into a lot bigger and fruitful organization than it was then.

Successful organizations are made by individuals who foster mutually beneficial suggestions between themselves, their providers and their clients. Be fair, legit and consistent with yourself. Try not to be voracious, don't be deceptive, be a decent pioneer. Great luck.

Rule 1 - If you can't sell, you're at a serious disadvantage.

"To find success in business you don't simply require a good thought - you need to sell it. Go ahead and sell. Try not to consider yourself everything except an advertiser." - Susan Sobbott, President, OPEN from American Express

A companion of mine began his own enrollment business, with extraordinary involvement with filling in as a venture supervisor and conveying all projects he oversaw on schedule and on spending plan, he longed for one day maintaining his own business, an effective enlistment firm. In the end, he pulled the trigger on the task the board job and began his own firm. He went through some cash on a logo, leased some office space in the city and started assembling a data set of faculty for which he could begin tracking down jobs. The issue was he was unable to offer anything to anybody; he simply wasn't a deals person.

Not just would he not sell anything, he be able to needed more cash to utilize an individual who could. So there he sat, after a couple of thump backs from the odd cold pitch he became firearm modest and inside half a month his business was finished. Presently you may be telling yourself that his disappointment was an aftereffect of lack of common sense and that he ought to know his assets and shortcomings and guaranteed he utilized individuals to fill the holes in his own capability. Indeed this is valid, however shouldn't something be said about in the event that circumstances get difficult and he was passed on to maintain the business alone. How is it that he could haul a business out of an opening assuming he can't sell anything?

The truth of start-up is there are times when you should battle it out alone, your salesman goes on leave or somebody stops. At some time, you are probably going to be expected to take care of business and begin selling. Not really to your clients either, raising capital requires the capacity to sell, while conversing with imminent financial backers in the event that you can't sell the blue sky you're simply not going to have the option to get the capital. Individuals put resources into individuals, especially while putting resources into start-ups.

As a forerunner in your new association you sell consistently, you offer to the clients, you offer to your representatives, you offer to your financial backers, and you even offer to your loan bosses. In the event that you can't sell, you are in a difficult spot. My recommendation to you is on the off chance that you can't sell, don't go solo. Observe yourself a colleague that can sell and go in to business with them. Look for accomplices that can fill your own ability holes, in the event that you can't sell, don't wrongly figure you can utilize assets to beat holes in your own capability during the foundation period of your business. Whenever your business dispatches it needs contributed individuals that can sell and market the business in each space they contact consistently. In the event that you're not an extrovert, better observe a colleague that is.

Peter Drucker once broadly said that business is two things: showcasing and development. He likewise commented that if either part is missing, there is no business. In the event that you're not honored with the endowment of the talk and you need to go into business then you should be a pioneer? You should be the one with the astounding thought, right?

Steve Wozniak and Steve Jobs made an extraordinary business association, albeit both of them cherished innovation and advancement it was obviously Jobs that was the marketeer in the business and Wozniak was the trailblazer. Apple is an illustration of two people who made a cooperative relationship where they perceived and utilized each other's assets to make a strong partnership.

So assuming you're generally the calm one at parties and are searching for an accomplice to help you with the foundation and activity of your new pursuit, begin your field-tested strategy and when you have finished it get on the web, promote for an accomplice, go to systems administration occasions and converse with bookkeepers. Bookkeepers know large number of business people who are continuously looking for opportunities.

If you are honored with the endowment of the chatter and can offer ice to the Eskimos, then maybe you really want a pioneer to assist you with executing your thought. Email me your subtleties and I will interface you for certain pioneers who frantically need an advertising partner.

Partners are an extraordinary method for circulating and share the gamble related with another endeavor. Assuming you have the cash, the assets and capacity to do it single-handedly, I emphatically exhort you do precisely that. Associations are a means to an end, just when they are necessary.

Rule 2 – Find yourself a Mentor

"Coaching is a cerebrum to pick, an ear to tune in, and a push in the correct heading." - John Crosby

A decent guide will be a resource for your business all through its whole lifecycle. During the thought and arranging period of your new beginning up, they can be a legit sounding board for your thoughts and market system hypothesis.

In 1994 I began fill in as a software engineer in Adelaide,

South Australia. The Company was called Global Communication Systems and it was a new company, a couple of months old. The organizer Gerry Follows had as of late relocated to Australia from Canada and had just been living in Adelaide for a couple of years. The organization was making and selling remote access phone cards for the hiker business in Australia. Following eighteen months the organization was offered to a rival in Melbourne.

The new organization who purchased Global offered me a job doing the exact thing I had been doing yet in their administrative center. Gerry was offered a job too, and in no time both of us got ourselves together and moved over to Melbourne. We shared a little unit together in Toorak, a sumptuous verdant suburb in Melbourne's east.

Before this time I hadn't actually had an over the top relationship with Gerry, expertly we got on well indeed and I appreciated working for him definitely. Nonetheless, in the new association I presently had another chief that I was answering to and the connection among Gerry and I moved from Boss and subordinate to companion and partner. After a brief timeframe, Gerry and I turned into the nearest of friends.

Over the years the connection among Gerry and I has gone from one solidarity to another. After the organization that purchased Global Communication Systems was put into liquidation, Gerry got back to Adelaide and I stayed in Melbourne where I shaped my first organization Smart Tec Corporation.

Since the finish of Global and that initial experience into my own business, Gerry has been an unbelievable Mentor. He has been sufficiently thoughtful to accept brings in the evening and assisted me with managing difficulties in my different organizations throughout the long term. Gerry has likewise been there to assist me studio thoughts for new organizations and we with having even established a business together in the property area. Despite the fact that he is currently resigned, he as of late flew down for a week and assisted me with managing some huge business

challenges I was confronting. Following twenty years we are as yet awesome of companions and converse with one another nearly daily.

When picking a coach you don't be guaranteed to have to choose someone from the business in which you are going to contend. Prior to beginning Global Communication Systems in the Telecommunications area Gerry had functioned as a Paramedic in Manitoba, Canada for close on 20 years. After Global, Gerry worked for Cable and Wireless, then Saab. Prior to resigning Gerry established a school for burdened youngsters known as the Same Program which was financed exclusively by the Christian Brothers. It was his assorted insight across various areas that made his recommendation so important to me. Gerry has a history of rehashing and adjusting to anything climate he thinks of himself as in, adjusting is something that each great business visionary will have to do while going into business. A savvy business person once let me know it is more essential to have close to zero insight into bunches of things than a great deal around one thing.

So my recommendation to you is observe a Mentor you regard, someone who has proactively accomplished what it is you are attempting to accomplish with your business. Ensure they are someone you can express your real thoughts to and someone you feel to which you can open up to. If conceivable, welcome your tutor on the excursion with you all along and take them with you each and every progression of the way. Ensure your tutor has the attributes, values and way of life to which you aspire.

It is presumably smart to formalize your functioning relationship with your guide and timetable ordinary catch ups. Ensure the gatherings are organized to guarantee that past activities and results are examined, new difficulties are shared and an open door exists to simply check in and talk about the here and now.

Use your guide as an underlying previously run center gathering for your thoughts in general and urge your tutor to offer a few thoughts of real value. Feature all of your hair cerebrum plans with them and truly flush out the preferences they have on any of the novel thoughts you are putting on the table.

Leverage their experience any place it very well might be and apply it to your business. Utilize your tutor as one more weapon in your munitions stockpile that you can release to assist you with accomplishing your objectives. Above all, take a gander at your
guide as your business coach.

Behind each extraordinary Athlete is a decent mentor. Since Roger Federer is the world's main tennis player doesn't mean he at this point not needs a mentor. The explanation Roger Federer has kept up with his number 1 positioning for such a long time is on the grounds that Roger comprehends the significance of having a decent mentor to assist with creating methodologies that dominate matches. Roger Federer is a tip top tennis player, his goal is to dominate tennis matches and huge homerun competitions. To find success you want to take a gander at yourself in a similar light, you are a world class financial specialist, your goal is to bring in cash and make riches. Roger Federer wouldn't enter Wimbledon without a mentor, nor would it be advisable for you enter an undertaking without a mentor either.

If you are to find true success, it is critical that you to have a decent mentor. A mentor that will work with you to foster systems that will assist you with accomplishing your objectives, be cutthroat, bring in cash and make wealth.

Rule 3 - Write your business plan, and then throw it out the window.

"not the arrangement is significant, it's the preparation." - Dr. Graeme Edwards

Since I am recommending that you toss your field-tested strategy through the window you should wonder why compose it? As far as I can tell, the genuine actual demonstration of composing the marketable strategy cover to cover is what's significant, not really the record you are left with. Albeit a decent strategy is a pre-imperative for raising capital, as the business person, it is the real actual composition of the strategy that is the initial move towards a fruitful beginning up business.

The test is in the event that you don't compose it, you won't ever know how you truly need to get your endeavor going. You would know how much cash you really want, what assets you really want, where you want to arrangement shop to lessen costs and be nearer to your market, what are your assets, shortcoming, open doors, dangers? What amount do you have to sell? When will you equal the initial investment? What will give you your upper hand? Until you really plunk down and begin expounding on this, you simply will not genuinely comprehend and really handle the critical difficulties and exertion that is going to face you.

Obviously the field-tested strategy is essential to raising capital and getting another endeavor supported, so you better ensure it is the hottest record you have composed throughout the year. Assuming you have never composed a marketable strategy get yourself one of those bit by bit directs. I utilize a manual called Anatomy of a Business Plan by Linda Pinson. Simply follow it page by page until it is finished, simple! Since utilizing the bit by bit guide, I can for the most part finish a decent field-tested strategy in a week.

When your strategy is finished, tie it or have it expertly printed. Ensure it has that wow factor and incorporates each conceivable situation and the fitting reaction that your future new company would be able and could at any point confront. I unequivocally suggest you additionally set up a going with show that gives a punchy significant level outline of your plan.

Now assuming you have completed it, you will have an extremely clear comprehension of how you will require and get your business going. Whenever you have raised your capital, enlisted your organization, recruited a couple of staff and got yourself some framework, tear the part entitled yearly financial plan out of the report and keep it not far off around your work area, toss the remainder of the record through the window, you will not be requiring it anymore.

Why would I want it any longer you inquire? Well from the day your business begins all that you thought you knew, all that you thought would occur, all that you accepted was a given without a doubt will not happen by any means. All things being equal, you will be confronted with a scope of various difficulties and interior and outside real factors that you won't ever consider. Prepare for the battle of your life. The day your endeavor goes live, you will begin developing, changing and adjusting to the real factors of your current circumstance. The main thing that is important in your field-tested strategy presently is obviously your gauge income explanation and financial plan. Better stick to it, being an unpleasant ride's going. Recall adjust or die.

Rule 4 - Hope for the best, plan for the worst

Many new companies that start with seed capital whether it be your own or a private backers capital frequently will more often than not experience the ill effects of beginning over dimensioning. Assuming you are entering an arising industry where your future rivals are now showing fantastic development and shocking incomes, it is a mix-up to accept that their world will turn into your own, unquestionably not quickly in any case. Numerous organizations have fallen in a load not long in the wake of beginning because of unreasonable estimate income assumptions at send off by its founders.

Whether you are endeavoring to repeat the achievement and favorable luck of a contender or you have what you accept to be an inconceivable item or administration that you can see will satisfy a current under overhauled hole inside a market, consistently embrace the view around your prosperity that you will accept it when you see it.

What number times have you been at a grill or a supper when you end up conversing with a beginning their own individual business and going on and on over on about how fruitful it will be and how much cash they will make? We have all been there. The degree of energy and fervor that comes from a great many people when it is practically infectious to start another business. Push ahead a couple of months and afterward you hear how it went under, couldn't raise sufficient capital, and was much harder than they naturally suspected it would have been, or you hear nothing at all.

I am an everlasting positive thinker, however I have taken in the most difficult way possible that you genuinely must stay cautiously optimistic, yet plan for terrible. This can be very troublesome when you are excessively hopeful and certain about your new pursuit. I realize I find this troublesome actually, as a critic I am not. It isn't in my tendency by any means. But it is imperative that you tighten up the reins on yourself, slow everything down and be conservative in your forecast projections and revenue in-flows.

Nobody at any point realizes what is around the bend. The greatest issue for business visionaries is that whenever troubles arise, they get rolling. Incomes are down, I want to work harder. Incomes are up, I really want to expand.

So numerous business visionaries wind up engaging it as far as possible, unfit to see that the dividers are crashing down around them. 'I simply need to change this here, change this there, fire that fellow and recruit someone else for that job, everything will be fine'. Assuming you end up putting out fires like this,
observe you want to make a move right away and be very definitive. Here and there when we are so focussed on accomplishing results, we overlook the present inward truth as our eyes are so immovably fixed on the prize.

During the beginning phases of start-up, a decent business person will deal with his income intently. The center should constantly be to get income positive today, not one week from now, not one year from now. The truth might be that the business won't be income positive until the following week, one month from now or one year from now however you should be working your business with the mentality that you are endeavoring to accomplish an income positive position today.

In the event that your business encounters an unexpected cataclysmic event, by ensuring that you are managing your costs, holding your cash where possible and running lean and mean, you will get through it.

Recently, I was operating a new online retail start up. The company had angel investors that were injecting capital into the business as needed until the business was self-sustaining. The business was performing well and doubling its revenues month on month. Ten months into the businesses operation, over another venture I was not involved in nor had visibility of the angel investors were sued and lost for $3 million dollars. The judgement consumed every dollar they had and suddenly without notice or warning my capital completely dried up. Suddenly I was in trouble and my internal environment was just flipped on its head.

This example demonstrates how you can never be sure of what is around the corner, those that are so focussed on the prize and growing the business to meet certain targets often find themselves the victim of an unforeseen cataclysmic event. As in the example given, some unforeseen events are impossible to plan for, that is why it is so important to hold on to your cash wherever possible.

It is important that every initiative, whether it be taking an office, renting a photo copier, hiring a person or opening a line of credit with a stationary supplier needs to be reviewed for risk. What is the risk? How do I mitigate the risk? How can I de-risk this transaction or engagement? If you review these three questions against every business decision you make, you're more likely to make a decision in such a way that reduces the risk and potential cost of that decision if your business encounters some significant challenges.

Rule 5 – Choose your partners wisely.

"Money motivates neither the best people, nor the best in people." – Dee Hock, Founder of Visa.

When seeking capital it is very difficult to be picky about your partners. Raising capital for a business that is multi-faceted with many internal and external dependencies is very challenging. Choosing the right partners can make this process even more difficult. It's true what they say, beggars can't be choosers.

When seeking venture capital, this rule seems impossible to adhere to, especially if you are a university student with an incredible idea and no money whatsoever. I am sure you would welcome anybody willing to put some much needed capital up to get your business off the ground, money is money.

Now this is going to cut to the core, but I must tell you and set an honest expectation with you. Your business is more likely going to completely crash and burn than be any kind of success. Better Be prepared for it when it comes and I seriously want you to focus on the word prepare. You need to ensure that when you setup and structure your business, you are the embodiment of a doomsday prepper always planning and preparing for disaster, because disaster, if it happens, is ugly. Be prepared, if you have silent partners, it can get even uglier.

It isn't all doom and gloom though, I personally have had more failures than successes when looking at the numbers of businesses I have worked in or started. However, I do believe that nothing is a failure if you learn something; my greatest successes were achieved through lessons learned from my greatest failures. When I first heard one of Australia's richest men say that 2 in every 3 businesses fail, I was so excited I almost leapt out of my chair. I had already failed in one business and was half way through getting my second venture off the ground. I knew that by these odds, I was either going to make it in this business or if I didn't the next one was going to be my crowning jewel!

If you are about to go into partnership of any kind of description you need to take a good hard look at the person or persons you are going into business with. You need to prepare for the fact that the relationship may turn sour, there may be arguments over money and if the shit hits the fan, it will be every man for himself.

Now if your partners are successful, wealthy and have a public profile and you are a complete nobody, then there is an imbalance of risk between you and your partners. You need to consider this when you structure your company, because if the business fails, you could find yourself on your own and up a creek without a paddle. If this day comes, if you're not prepared for it life as you know it will be over, at least for a while.

Firstly, you need to realise that people investing capital in your new venture, are investing in you. Sure you might have a great product or service but any successful business is the result of good organisational architecture and execution. If you fail in either of these two factors and you have left your investors exposed, get ready for hell fire and brimstone.

When reviewing potential investment partners, the first step is to look at how you can protect your investors in the event that the business fails. It is important to realise that your investors don't care about the company and they likely don't share your passion for the brand and your love of the industry. They probably don't get warm and fuzzy about all your achievements and the amazing corporate culture you have created. They more than likely only care about one thing, a return on their investment. If you don't deliver a return, they won't be looking at the market or the external or internal realities that led to the cash flow decline. If the business fails your investors won't make allowances for a down turn in the global economy or the sudden increase in competition, the finger of blame will be pointed solely at you.

Let us just move forward to a potential Armageddon scenario. Imagine it with me if you will. You have burned through the total amount your investors have contributed, you have had your head down and your arse up furiously working to turn it around, you have been robbing Peter to pay Paul, creditors are getting angry and calling non-stop, customers are screaming at you, you don't have enough money to pay staff. You haven't paid yourself for months, the media is calling to get a statement regarding several complaints they have received regarding your business from customers and suppliers. Your broke, the tax man is calling because you haven't been making your regular payments. This particular scenario is the typical situation for small businesses prior to being placed into voluntary administration or worst, liquidation

Well what would you do now? Now if you have not correctly structured your company so your partners are protected, and they too are now getting heat from the media, creditors and the like, what you should expect is an assault from all sides. Your investors will seamlessly transition from partners to creditors, and unlike you they have money and loads of it.

The investor's lawyers get involved; if their investment is secured over you they just become another creditor and go after your house. If they are listed as company directors and have begun receiving nasty calls from creditors and the like, they are going to try and distance themselves from ground zero as quickly as possible. Before you know it, you will be left holding the baby with no money to defend yourself against the onslaught that is going to send you into bankruptcy and worst, if you traded while insolvent potential criminal charges. Many successful and high profile business people have found themselves on the wrong side of the law due to insolvency trading matters.

So if you are looking at launching your venture with some investor capital, better start doomsday prepping now.

If the investors want to sit on the board, perfect! This is great because you can utilise their skill and experience to collectively make decisions that take the business forward. See your accountant to implement a structure for them that during the initial phase of the company's establishment gives them the ownership and security they are after, as well as the input they require to be comfortable into the day to day running of the business. Most of all, setup a directorship structure to ensure their commercial reputation and public profile cannot be compromised in the event of company failure. Doing so won't just be for protecting them but you will be protecting yourself also.

Special purpose entities for investors are a great way to shield them from issues that arise when a business becomes insolvent and goes into administration or liquidation. A special purpose entity for your investors is less likely to have an impact on any of their other commercial interests.

Ask your accountant to structure your partner's investment as an unsecured loan or capital in return for shares. Be sure that you don't find yourself as a minority shareholder, you could find yourself in a situation where you have no control over the company and you become the servant of your investors. Be sure to structure the capital so if the company completely crashes and burns, they are completely unsecured and are one less creditor you need worry about.

Ideally your start-up business partner should be a person who has roughly the same amount of money as you, the same public profile and a similar external situation as you. Being in business with a person who shares the same wants and needs regarding the business as you do means that you are more likely to collectively work through any issues together. When it is mutually beneficial for you both to achieve the same outcome, things will just work a lot easier.

The other factor about choosing a partner who is from the same socio-economic demographic as you are, you are more likely to persevere longer with your business than investors will. When an investor has injected capital into a business and sees their investment slipping away, the last thing they will want to do is invest any more. Keep this in mind too when considering wind up costs in your business plan.

Finally, if you are selecting a working equal partner who will work the business shoulder to shoulder with you, be sure to select a partner who has the appropriate skills and capability to fulfil their role. Ensure that all partners' responsibilities and accountabilities within the business are clear and that your chosen partners have the competence required to successfully perform their function. You don't want to find out too late that they don't have the skills required; you will end up doing your role and theirs if you're not careful.

Rule 6 - Got an exit strategy? No? Then get one...

"Every exit is an entry somewhere else." – Tom Stoppard

Exit strategies are often overlooked in business plans and usually left as a small paragraph or footnote at the end of the document which usually mentions selling the business or floating the business on the stock exchange. Most entrepreneurs starting their first venture anticipate the business being a raging success and see themselves at the helm of the business as it grows into a large multi-national, why would you need an exit strategy with all this money rolling in?

'I once heard a leading business expert state that if you have an exit strategy in your business plan then you must not be passionate enough about your business.'

I believe that increased focus needs to be given on the exit strategy in the initial planning and setup stage of the business. I also believe that you need more than one exit strategy, an exit strategy designed for every possible exit scenario.

By having a good handle on your exit scenario options, you will know when and where which exit strategy should be executed. A solid understanding of your exit strategy scenarios will ensure that you start planning your exit the day you start your new venture. Exit strategies are your plan B, having three or even more exit strategies will ensure you have Plan C, Plan D and so on and so forth.

It is imperative that you have an exit plan in place for your investors, when will their investment mature? How do you plan for them to exit? How do they want to exit? Do they wish to exit with an option to re-invest?

Your exit plan options must be based on performance targets, if your company fails to hit performance target A, then execute exit Plan B. If your company hits Performance Target B, then begin the implementation of exit Plan C and so on and so forth.

For example, let's just discuss the idea of your industry taking an overall downturn, the bubble you have been operating in is bursting and the solution is competitor consolidation or sale of your business. Your company's performance targets have fallen below the expected revenue levels and this level of revenue at this time of your business is a trigger for you to implement exit strategy C, sell the business or merge and consolidate.

By having triggers in place based on performance targets, you will always be aware when and where an exit strategy plan must be executed. This will ensure you are not caught off guard by acting too late. As each exit strategy is based on achieving a financial and commercial outcome, a good range of exit strategies based on company performance variables is the best way of protecting yourself, your investment and your investor's capital. Those that don't have a good understanding of exit strategies find themselves suffering from too little to late syndrome. By the time they realise they need to exit, they no longer have the money, the resources and the time to successfully execute a plan. The outcome for them is a fire sale of their business and assets if they are lucky.

Know yourself. Always keep at the forefront of your mind why you started your business in the first place. Understand what it is that you wanted to achieve and structure your exit strategies accordingly. Whether you want to achieve a certain monetary figure, an amount of money that you and your family could live comfortably on could be one trigger for your exit strategy. Having clearly defined exit strategy goals makes the act of achieving these goals more structured, focussed and more likely to succeed.

Rule 7 - Trust your intuition, but don't believe your own hype.

Now I don't profess to be an expert on the human psyche, most of the time people I know leave me scratching my head as I witness some of the commercial decisions they make in their business life, particularly when it comes to people. If a person is the sum total of their life's experiences and it is these experiences which influence their decisions, depending on what kind of life they have lived will probably have a direct result on the kind of life they lead.

When somebody is starting a new venture, the excitement, the enthusiasm and the belief that it will be a huge success almost becomes a fantasy and more often than not they start believing their own hype. Once ego gets involved people start believing they are experts at everything and masters of the universe. If you think that you have got it all worked out, guess what, you have started believing your own hype.

They say that success is a combination of some talent and a whole lot of luck, the challenge is that people have a tendency to get the percentages mixed up and start believing that the luck component was a direct result of their talent. When this happens they start attributing their success to 100% talent and luck has nothing to do with it. Whenever I hear somebody say you create your own luck, I know that they have fallen victim to their own hype.

A new business is exciting, after all if you didn't think it was going to be a success you wouldn't have started it. What is important to understand is why you are starting it. I once had a friend who was so eager to be a self-employed successful business man that he got involved in a business with a friend that he knew nothing about at all and it just about ended him. Before embarking on your own business you need to understand what it is that drives you.

My friend's desire to establish a new business was driven by the romantic view he had of himself as a successful entrepreneur, not the desire to make a successful business but the desire to enjoy the lavishes of fame and fortune, the cars, the houses, the clothes and so on and so forth. His desire to achieve this social position in the community was so strong he would have sold everything he had and invested in anything that even gave him a glimmer of hope that this lifestyle that he dreamed of could be achieved. When his friend had discussed his start up business venture idea and positioned it as a sure thing, my friend was on the phone to the bank manager within minutes mortgaging his house so he could invest.

Is there such a thing as a sure thing? The only sure thing in life is that you get what you pay for.

Now personal values are a funny thing, you don't know you have them until it comes time to compromise them. Sure, we would all like to think that we are all good, honest, God fearing people but when it comes down to the wire, you don't really know what you would do in a certain situation until you are truly faced with the choice. We all however get inclinations of our values from time to time, feelings and reactions that cause us to stop, take stock and look closer into a situation. I tend to refer to this as my intuition.

If something doesn't feel right, whether you are potentially recruiting somebody, going into a business partnership or even just walking into a bar, in my experience if your intuition tells you to stop, then you better stop. Your values are your own personal view of what's right or wrong, wherever they come from I firmly believe they are designed to protect you. They are part of the fight or flight mechanism that each one of us has somehow engraved into our DNA. Values and instinct are invariably linked, and they somehow alert you at a subconscious level that something is not quite right, you become alert, you pause, you take stock, you choose.

Now greed and desire are the sworn enemies of your values and instinct. If the sum total of your personal values and instinct manifests itself as intuition, how often have you found yourself saying my intuition said no, but I did it anyway and now look where I am? More often than not your intuition just lost out to desire or greed and now you are paying the price for it. It may not be so bad in day to day life if you rarely trust your intuition, you go out with the wrong girl or guy, buy the wrong cheese or go and see a bad movie, but if you don't listen to your intuition in business it could end you. If your intuition says no, you better listen. If a decision needs to be made on the spot and your intuition says no, but your greed or desire says yes, delay the decision until you have had time to think it through properly. You will thank yourself for the restraint later.

How often have you recruited somebody just to find after he started he was terrible, lazy, didn't have a clue? Did you find during the interview process that he knew all the right things to say, was ticking all the boxes but your intuition just said no? I have been in this exact situation before and due to a complete and utter lack of alternative applicants I hired an individual as he met the required criteria. Sure enough, turns out the guy could talk the talk but as my intuition told me, he couldn't walk the walk.

If something doesn't feel right, then don't do it. It might give the idea that you are falling short on other options yet you will see as one, and you will find one that feels right. Trust your instinct, as it is your sub-cognizant addressing you, it is your very own worth framework attempting to speak with you. Those that don't listen quite often experience the consequences.

Rule 8 - Bootstrap, bootstrap, bootstrap

"A chicken doesn't quit scratching since worms are scant." - Grandma's Axiom.

Run your business on a shoelace, consistently. It is so natural when you are going into business to get out there and make the most unbelievable work place the world has at any point seen. Clearly any on the web or actual regions that will be client confronting should be lovely, rousing and urge individuals to burn through cash. At every possible opportunity however, consistently hope to track down approaches to bootstrap.

Need a few work areas, eBay. Need a few PCs, online closeout locales. Need a telephone framework, track down a recycled one. Need a board room table or organization gear, consistently purchase second-hand. In the event that clients don't come to your office, don't put a sign up. Besides assuming no clients will at any point come to your office who cares where your office will be!

Now there is a great deal to be said about how a decent work place assists increment with staffing yield. Bootstrapping doesn't imply that you will have everyone working in a climate that doesn't advance joint effort or difficult work, yet it implies that you can save a couple of bucks purchasing resources that will be worth the very same sum when you sell them as though you purchased pristine gear from a business office originator warehouse.

Get the staff in question, reward staff who support the obtaining of vital resources that address the issues of the association without burning through every last cent. It simply doesn't need to connect with assets.

Several years prior I was dealing with an enormous group of

Telecommunication engineers. Because of some innovation stage changes there turned into a critical need to prepare the staff on the most proficient method to utilize Oracle information bases. Whenever I rang a preparation association, I was cited $1300 per individual to have the preparation expected given to the staff. With 23 staff this planned to cost me $29,900. Rather than proceeding with preparing from the enrolled preparing association, I called a spotter and inquired as to whether they had any jobless up-and-comers who had insight with Oracle preparing. Sure enough they did and I got a person to come into the workplace and train all our staff for just $45 each hour. The complete preparation for every one of the 23 staff just wound up costing me $1800, an immense saving of $28,100.

Bootstrapping doesn't have to simply apply to office gear or preparing. You can apply it to anything. A couple of years prior an organization I was running in the property business took a choice over a bundle of land, before

we had paid the choice charge we discovered that the land proprietor had proactively applied for the very sort of advancement on the property that we planned to do and their application for improvement had been unsuccessful.

The agreement we had marked was unshakable in the seller's approval, so it was absolutely impossible that we could try not to pay the choice expense despite the fact that we didn't need the land any longer. Presently the choice expense was just $10,000, yet when I attempted to renege on the installment, they sent their legal counselor after me and a letter of interest. The issue for me was I had no cash for a legal counselor myself and I truly required that 10k to get a choice on another property. Attorneys charge continuously, and they don't come modest. So I set out on a correspondence program with their attorney that happened day to day, I would call him consistently and in a real sense bother him for an over hour. By day 4 the merchant of the land pulled out the interest on the choice installment and we left the arrangement. By bootstrapping along these lines, I was expanding their legitimate bill consistently by an hour and costing them cash to pursue me, I was having a good time I hadn't started to carry out the other expense expanding drives I had available for them.

Effective bootstrapping can be applied to nearly anything assuming that you develop, make a stride back and check what is going on out. To practically any expense a business should bring about there is generally a minimal expense boot lashing arrangement, and recollect whether you don't require it now, you don't require it now.

Rule 9 - Only employ super stars!

"Ability dominates matches, however cooperation and knowledge comes out on top for titles." - Michael Jordan

It is difficult to take off like a bird when you are fluttering around with a lot of turkeys.

You could have the best item and business thought the world has at any point known yet assuming that you have a group of morons supporting the execution of your endeavor, just take it all in it go totally no place. I like to allude to HR as human resources. It is valid what they say that the genuine resource of an association is in its people.

Now the test with employing hotshots is there is a suspicion that they don't come modest. I have worked in numerous enormous associations and I have in my opportunity arrive across many generously compensated people who were plainly awkward inside their job. We have all been there, asking ourselves, how did they get this job? Who hired this clown? How is it that they are still working here? Large corporate organisations are full of individuals who instead of getting fired get moved around and promoted so they become other people's problems. Actually imbeciles cost a fortune also.

So assuming your new pursuit is inside a laid out industry, you have the test of industry normalized benchmarks for most jobs you wish to fill. You really must just recruit quality individuals, huge companies are spending a fortune attempting to get this right these days with different screenings, surveys, drug tests and psychometric testing. If you don't have the money and the resources to poke and prod your candidates until you are 100% satisfied then you need to establish ways to get the same outcomes achieved by your large corporate brethren without spending the money.

Be responsibility phobic. Feel free to begin someone on a transient agreement with the perspective on moving to a full time job, like that in the event that they don't work out you can have them leave the business and stay away from overt repetitiveness expenses, punishments and leave privileges. Assuming they back themselves they will cheerfully concur. If they are not willing to come over without some kind of permanent security, then they are more than likely not going to be a good fit anyway.

Try pretending with them, acquire another staff part and request that they carry on assuming they are in a deals job, or to deliver a piece of work that is applicable to the job they have applied for. It's anything but something troublesome for them to do in the event that they are proficient and will offer them the chance to demonstrate

their capability.

Always interview them two times, ensure no less than 3 days separated. That way you have opportunity and willpower to reflect as will they and you get a further an open door to get to realize them better at any rate. By meeting them something like two times you will wind up with as long as two hours of genuine conversation about their abilities, assets, shortcomings and capability.

Understand their assets, center around their assets. Guarantee that the job they are applying for is ideal for their assets. Audit their shortcomings, assuming the job they are going for incorporates capacities that they are clearly showing a soft spot for, disregard employing them. Continuously work individuals to their assets and not their shortcomings. The No. 1 rule for making Superstars in the work environment is making a solid match between the individual and the function.

Look for capable, green and hungry people over war fatigued dinosaurs. You'll get twofold the value for your money and people who are quick to learn and make a name and notoriety for themselves. Assuming you utilize another person's hotshot you could end up in a steady conflict of wills with a person who accepts they know best the way in which things ought to be done and will battle you like there's no tomorrow until they get their way.

Always look for people who show innovative soul and drive, their contribution to your endeavor will be unlimited over the long haul. Utilize brilliant, road shrewd individuals who have figured out how to hook their direction through college or through private difficulties in spite of a family separate or passing in the family. These kinds of people will lift to any test whenever difficulties arise. Ask them what individual difficulties they have needed to look in their lives.

Finally, prior to settling on any choice ask yourself this, "would I be able to work with this individual? Will this individual assist me with accomplishing my objectives?" If the response is indeed, and above all your instincts say OK then you have without a doubt found yourself a winner.

Rule 10 - Grow your business in line with your

revenue

"Everybody discusses developing the business, yet what you don't hear enough about is the significance of not developing the business excessively quick." - Blue Man

Sometimes you really want to develop to get by; once in a while you really want to develop to contend. There is in inner strain for a beginning up among development and cost. Development might additionally expand your item offering, more items, more noteworthy topographical reach, yet development can likewise eat into your edges, require more prominent assets to oversee and additionally increment your functional costs.

You might have seen that dissimilar to other business person distributions my first rule isn't the standard disrupt every one of the principles guideline. You can't disrupt every one of the guidelines, yet a few implicit standards are unquestionably there for the breaking.

I am certain you are asking yourself, 'what are the implicit principles'? Well they are there and there are large number of them across each industry type. As a first time business person the primary implicit decide that you are probably going to go over is the one encompassing enterprises and human resources costs.

Created by teams of industry specific recruitment specialists and perhaps even unions in some countries salary bench marks are a great way to ensure that resources with particular skills get the most income they can earn for their industry type. It is obviously an extraordinary way for ventures with different players to plot to guarantee their human resources costs doesn't surpass industry levels thus they can't poach workers off one another. Football crews attempt to work like this yet incidentally some group penetrates the compensation cap.

If you are entering another industry, you would accept that it be suitable that you enlist industry experts who have the extraordinary ability sets you expect to make your business a triumph. 'Poach the top business folks from your opposition and recreate their progress in your endeavor appears to be a gamble free way to progress?' The supposition that being that the business standard rates could be the genuine expense for the HR you require.

The question you need to ask yourself before you hire industry specialists is why? Why do I need this person? What value will this person bring to my business? What problem can this person fix? Is it competence? Is it a network? Customers? A corporate culture? If you asking yourself this then perhaps it is time to break the unspoken rule.

MySpace was the person to person communication monster of the mid 2000's, with a great many individuals it developed at a disturbing rate and in 2005 was bought by News Corp for an astounding $580 million dollars. Presently we as a whole have heard

the term distinct advantages and MySpace turned into the survivor of a distinct advantage inside its industry and in 2011 the organization was sold for a measly $35 million in contrast with its unique deal cost. The distinct advantage was obviously Facebook; Facebook offered a cleaner more creative stage for virtual entertainment and thus spread virally across the web and consumed MySpace's whole piece of the pie in the process.

If you have a business that isn't a syndication inside a specific industry, you should be a distinct advantage. Because if you aren't, somebody else will be and you can be certain that it is likely to be an unforeseen cataclysmic event for you. The issue with recruiting staff straightforwardly from your rivals is that when individuals run over, they work precisely as they accomplished for your rival. Why not, it's functioned admirably for them. The issue here is that you're not changing the game. You are simply reproducing your rivals business and approaches to working and expecting to make similar progress as they have.

If you are attempting to reenact your rivals you can have confidence that you are not changing the game and you are probably going to come up short. As your rivals have the advantage of first mover over you and are now encountering the difficulties of their outer climate and answering as needs be. You then again will just gain proficiency with their illustrations long after they have pushed ahead, they are the ones who will turn into the distinct advantage to your business and you will be basically straying behind.

They say the most limited distance between two focuses is a straight line. I once began an internet based day to day bargain business and ran it for more than a year prior being compelled to close the business. It was another industry for myself and I had no clue about how existing contenders were getting the arrangements they were getting to sell on their site to their enrollment base. I hopped on LinkedIn and began conversing with key sales reps who were working for my rivals and obviously comprehended the arrangement securing process personally. Over espresso with these people I was flabbergasted no sweat of how they procured these arrangements, how bargain obtaining was about private connections and how the most any salesman could probably accomplish was 2 arrangements a week.

My rivals had groups of sales reps meeting with eatery proprietors, rub administrators and lodging administrators arranging arrangements to be sold on contender destinations. They worked away from the workplace and invested a ton of their

energy going between potential Merchants creating connections, getting their business and arranging bargains. Whenever I asked how much would they need to join my new beginning up association the compensations they were requesting to move was so extreme my capital would be exhausted before I even started!

When I moved toward different deals staff from various contenders I viewed them all as working the same way, if I needed to have one new deal a day in each capital city over five capital cities I was going to need a minimum of 3 sales staff per capital city meaning of course I would have to recruit 15 sales staff to successfully have a daily deal site that is competitive in the space. The salary levels of course had been set by my competition and benchmarked accordingly so my human capital costs for these people was going to be so high it created significant cost risk if the business didn't achieve enough revenue to sustain the work force.

My test was clear before me, I expected to develop my business rapidly by upgrading my labor force right away. Assuming that I planned to contend I wanted however many arrangements as my rivals and the same amount of topographical inclusion. My capital was restricted however; I was unable to stand to employ sufficient industry experienced deals people.

Maybe my predicament was really a chance for me to change the game.

'How is it that I could change the game', I wondered?

I was unable to manage the cost of many experienced staff, assuming I was going to compete
against the large young men I must set up serious arrangements, on the off chance that I would have been fruitful I was reasonable must set up more arrangements and more ideal arrangements consistently to draw in the clients. Without capital for 15 deals staff at the present going rate it would have been hard to recreate my rivals offering.

By chance I found myself at a dinner with friends where I met a sales person who was working for Yellow Pages; they informed me that all Yellow Pages sales teams did all their sales work over the phone and everything was cold calling and lead handling. This was the arrangement! Assuming that I utilized phone salespeople at a cheaper I could accomplish higher change rates because of the more productive utilization of time. No longer would deals staff squander time
making a trip from one Merchant to another for an up close and personal gathering, a call would be made, on the off chance that a deal couldn't be accomplished with one Merchant they essentially hung up the telephone and called another Merchant.

It was a revelation; I promptly began selecting minimal expense phone salespeople and set them to work. I worked intimately with them to additionally foster the contents and the snares expected to finish bargains. Before two weeks' over at the cost of one of my rivals deals staff I could bear the cost of 3 phone salespeople, my transformation rates were going through the rooftop and in no time my phone outreach groups were each accomplishing at least 2 arrangements each day. The outcome was I had a much cheaper base than my rivals and had a more prominent number of arrangements accessible to my clients. Whenever I sent off I was the distinct advantage and my rivals didn't have any idea what hit them, it was interesting it is the way to watch them reproducing me.

Innovation. By employing phone salespeople rather than account administrators, I had disrupted the un-verbally expressed norm. I had split away from this industry patterns connecting with bargain obtaining and subsequently I had decreased my expense base and accomplished more with less. The outcome was lower functional expenses and a more noteworthy item proposing to my clients. Assuming that you are taking a gander at developing your business ask yourself, how might it be improved, less expensive and with less assets? By taking a gander at my enrollment needs uniquely in contrast to the business standard, I had the option to develop the business past industry assumptions and be more serious in the process.

Firstly however, comprehend what you can manage. How are your deals moving? Is it safe to say that they are moving up? Take a gander at your information, are your deals conjectures in accordance with how they were moving a year ago? What's going on the lookout? Alright, so you might have had a decent week however that is too little an example to pursue choices with respect to expanding the expenses of your business now. Had a good month? Had a good two months? Seeing good revenue growth? Can your business comfortably absorb the cost associated with the growth now or are you relying on the additional operational resources to create the revenue you need to sustain them? If your business cannot absorb the addition of the proposed operating cost now then you cannot justify the expense.

If not extending isn't a choice, but rather you simply don't have the money for additional functional expense increments then you want to check out at your present functional expenses and cycles. On the off chance that you want to extend however you don't have the

income to assimilate the extra costs then you really want to take a gander at what you have now that you can dispose of. Can I perform that function myself? Can I distribute that process across multiple resources? Can I outsource that function to a lower cost service or solution? You need to cut and trim where possible to free up the necessary cash to expand and grow, never embrace the conviction that assuming you assemble it they will come with regards to extension and income. On the off chance that you can't bear the cost of it now you can't have it.

The way to effective extension comes from solid income the executives and concentration and functional proficiency. For a beginning up activity bring costs into the business when the income is free to support them. Solid spotlight on functional productivity and development will guarantee you are maintaining your business as lean and mean as could really be expected and therefore, you will without a doubt have all suitable money available for any business extension you require.

Rule 11 - Always pay yourself first.

Heard the colloquialism assuming you care for yourself everyone benefits? Assuming you are having income issues out of the blue, a circumstance that is generally normal with any new company guarantee that you pay yourself first before any other person. It is truly challenging to maintain a business effectively assuming you are battling to take care of the bills at home.

Now we as a whole comprehend that a decent pioneer generally puts the necessities of his kin before his own however that doesn't work in business. Assuming the business flounders, fizzles, requires scaling down, goes into organization or sells you will in any case be there. As far as possible until the hopeless end, regardless of what. It's your child; it's your obligation in happy times and in terrible. Workers can simply leave, they can land another position, they can continue on. Not you however, you're stuck there as far as possible. So pay yourself as long as you can, focus on your compensation over any remaining workers and lenders. On the off chance that you don't, when everything turns out badly you won't just be wrapping up your organization, you will likewise be taking a gander at moving your family in with your folks, or worse.

Rule 12 - Always assume that everyone is going to try and rip you off.

I once had a person I was ready to go with let me know point dark, that your either the one doing the screwing or the one being in a bad way. Assuming anyone you're working with at any point expresses that to you, figure out how to screw them over right away or made tracks. I wish I had done both of those things. Enough about me anyway.

One thing I have learnt in my somewhat short life is that cash draws out the most terrible in individuals. I have had loan bosses that I have created mind blowing kinships with just to have them turn on me like crazy canines when I was late for a payment.

If you understand that cash draws out the most exceedingly terrible in individuals then comprehend this, individuals who are ready to go and who are fruitful are driven by cash. They love it, they need a greater amount of it and they are typically plotting and conspiring on how they can clutch what they have procured and track down ways of acquiring more, parcels more. The best cash at any point got was cash you never worked for and there are dependably individuals attempting to make a fast and simple buck, the most straightforward buck is acquired by swindling a clueless individual.

Trust no one, if a transaction you are involved in carries even the slightest potential risk of you losing your grip on your money and not receiving anything for it, then don't proceed. Continuously find a way to de-risk any exchange, whether it being purchasing stock, paying representatives ahead of time or opening up a credit represent a client. Money is difficult to earn and even harder to hold on to. Pay nothing except if you have some security that the exchange will be finished with respect as you would prefer, assuming you should pay ahead of time for labor and products pay stores at any rate and the excess equilibrium upon receipt of exchanges. For abroad buys use credit notes and global planned operations suppliers, be cautious, be careful and totally emphatically trust no one.

Rule 13 - Don't develop your marketing plan until you know who your customer is.

"The timely riser might get the worm, yet the subsequent mouse gets the cheddar." - Unknown.

Ever heard the term 'delicate send off' or 'beta delivery'? These are terms instituted by enormous effective associations who discharge an item for audit to a restricted crowd. Too many new businesses wrongly talk with showcasing associations while their item is in the improvement stage, promoting organizations inventive groups will go to work and amaze you with story sheets and models of TV ads, print articles, mottos and get cry's that will get you so invigorated you will toss cash at them to get it going. This is a horrendous slip-up, assuming you are going to send off an item and you are meeting with a showcasing organization, stop what you are doing, close your look at book and walk. Let them know you will be back later.

If you are about to release your product to the world, then you better start thinking about your soft launch or beta release. First and foremost, attempt and comprehend how you could play out a delicate send off. Where is your audience? Who is your audience? Where do they live? What do they do? How do you find them? Now these are issues that your marketing company will tell you they will resolve with their sharp and sassy campaign but it won't work. It will just cost you a huge load of cash and leave you thinking about what went wrong.

I had an individual involvement in one of Melbourne's driving promoting firms. We were fostering an item that was explicitly made for the female segment. At the hour of my organizations early foundation, there was just myself and two different men arranging the organization. The showcasing firm proposed this astonishing promoting effort that comprised of a lady with a horrendous samurai blade cutting costs on all that we were doing. The TV advertisement was themed after Kill Bill and the three of us folks totally adored it, thought it had shock esteem, was something truly unique and was somewhat hot moreover. We were so energized we transferred ownership of an actually take a look at straight. Three weeks into pre-creation I showed the story board to a couple of ladies, they tracked down the ridiculous sword grim, bloody and obnoxious and didn't feel constrained or inquisitive to draw in with the brand any further. I pulled the trigger quickly on the mission, three people and one of Melbourne's driving advertising organizations had come up short totally, getting the mix-up early implied we got off delicately. In the event that I hadn't delicate sent off the mission with my market segment we would have been done before we even started.

If you have any comprehension of your potential market segment, welcome others to survey your item. Try not to stop there; request that they audit your image, logo and some other deals content. Request veritable criticism; pay them on the off chance that you need to. Figure out who likes it, who could do without it. If you find that a certain gender or age demographic likes your product more than another, then they are your market. Take a gander at what different organizations promoting to that segment are doing, and imitate crusades that are working.

Ask for certifiable input on your item, what did they like about it? What didn't they like? Make changes where you really want to, continue onward until your segment is fulfilled and partakes in your item. Really at that time are you prepared, take all your delicate send off notes and criticism and head on back to that showcasing organization, you currently have the scholarly capital expected for an effective promoting effort, feel free to place it into action.

What makes a hit melody is a snare, that one piece of the tune which compels it to split away from the pack and be a main hit. It is typically a short riff, an entry or expression that simply sucks individuals in and makes them need to hear it again and again. Like a diagram besting melody, an effective mission needs a snare simply the same.

Now anyone with an advertising degree will let you know that you really want move around procedures inside your showcasing effort. Push strategies are strategies such as television and radio that push messages about your product and brand to your market, pull strategies are strategies that engage directly with your potential customers and draw them directly or incentivise them to your product or service.

Getting there consideration is a certain something, augmenting the open door is something else through and through various. Great promoting will carry clients to your entryway, your shop or your site however assuming you don't have anything on offer they are keen on at that specific time, the second they leave you have lost the client forever.

In this day and age everyone is associated through the web, online organizations successfully use email as an approach to straightforwardly speaking with their clients. Regardless of what business you are in, compelling utilization of email direct showcasing can help you in driving deals, expanding income and keep up with direct commitment with your customers.

Your promoting effort ought to then have the accompanying attributes, it ought to really impart what your identity is, what you do and why you are unique, it ought to successfully convey your image, item and administration. It should include a component that effectively brings people to your business and lastly it should contain a hook that gives you the ability to capture information of the customer or potential customer so you can keep communicating with them long after they have left your store, online webpage or office.

Get prepared for your launch!

Rule 14 – If you can't scale your business up, welcome to your new job!

One of the normal downfalls of whenever business person first is the inability to incorporate adaptability into their business frameworks. One of my very first workers proceeded to begin his own special firm. Being a gifted creator who was use to investing wholeheartedly in his work, he utilized his abilities to make a mind blowing portfolio and resume of work. Albeit unfit to figure out full opportunity business, he began building a customary client base who he worked with to foster sites and other inventive print material.

Every time I see him he is really buckling down in the business, early morning begins and late evenings working almost to excess irately to get the work out so he can begin the following position. Standing ready is a size of work having a place with eager clients who all needed it finished yesterday.

"How about you get some assistance?" I asked him on numerous occasions.

"It is elusive great assistance, my work is known to be of the greatest quality and I can't invest my energy repairing awful work to guarantee it meets my high plan standards!"

"Yet your clients are discontent with the postponements, you have stir stacking up", I shouted, "You plainly need help!"

Therefore, my companion frequently loses clients. He shows up on Saturday or Sunday to attempt to get on top of it. The issue is it simply continues to stack up and with next to no powerful business frameworks set up he ends up in a ceaseless circle working starting with one work then onto the next for keeps in sight.

With all the minimal expense work coming from arising innovation nations, for example, India and China, I once went to him and inquired "how about you re-appropriate a portion of your work to China?"

"Gracious the Chinese", he answered, "They can't do quality plan like I
can!"

My companion was shut to novel thoughts; overseeing additional individuals was an unfamiliar idea. He firmly had faith in his own image and couldn't separate his business from his image. My companion obviously isn't a financial specialist. He opened his own firm since he couldn't get a new line of work; through informal exchange he landed little plan positions every now and then. As informal spread and he started creating associations with different firms,   he

began helping more work through verbal. Next thing he realized he had his very own business, he is a coincidental businessman.

If you can't build scalability into your business, then you don't have a business. You have effectively made yourself a task. The contrast between being a business visionary and being a professional is the capacity to foster frameworks that will make scale. The capacity to grow the assets and ability of the business without losing quality or time. As a matter of fact, viable business frameworks ought to present efficiencies, empowering a business to convey more at better caliber and in less time!

If my companion was a business visionary, he might seaward the plan work to his organization. Then create a system for effectively managing the effort and quality of the work coming from the off shore teams. He would foster innovation to guarantee work survives from the best and standard. That way he may as yet charge a premium and convey an exceptional quality item without having the accumulation of stir stacking up from his clients. Truth be told, on the off chance that he could foster the innovation and frameworks to really oversee configuration groups seaward, he could scale his business straight up, open highway workplaces, open worldwide workplaces or even make franchises!

This is the contrast between being an Entrepreneur and being an inadvertent money manager. Assuming you are flying performance and are content with your business how it is, well you might have made some work for yourself that gives you incredible adaptability, extraordinary hours yet sadly no wiped out pay or occasion pay.

However, if you are interested in building a company, creating an organisation and expanding and scaling up your business, then ask yourself this, 'how can this be done through other resources without sacrificing quality?' 'Can this be achieved quicker and at a lower cost if I develop technology, systems or processes?'

Building frameworks that give a business scale will make consistently duplicating income channels that will dramatically develop your organization's profit. The formation of frameworks and cycles intended to increase a business will prompt the improvement of groups and genuine enduring achievement is just accomplished with and through teams.

Rule 15 - If you're new to the industry, call your competitors and say Hi.

"Rivalry has been demonstrated to be helpful in a measured way and no further, however participation, which is what we should take a stab at today, starts where contest leaves off." - Franklin D. Roosevelt

People love discussing themselves, especially on the off chance that you're on a point they are energetic about. On the off chance that your new pursuit is the most up to date contestant into a specific market, call your rivals and present yourself.

Be striking as well, ask them how they got their market position, what they see the business doing from here on out and how might they advance their business going ahead. In the event that you don't ask, you don't get.

I once rang the market chief in a section I was working in and he spent an hour on the phone discussing how he had accomplished their market driving position, the difficulties they looked during foundation and later activity and where he saw the business heading from now on. It was a smart conversation and one that occurred through my capacity to construct moment compatibility and present myself as a non-threat.

Keep the lines of correspondence open, assuming a provider consumes you call your rivals and let them know. Exhibit that despite the fact that you're in contest, you have faith in sound rivalry and don't have any desire to see them getting scorched by awful players in the market space. On the off chance that there is nothing accessible, take a gander at making industry discussion bunches where you can share data and in general work together to foster the business as a whole.

The main explanation however for these connections are not all the babble I just referenced in the past passages. Your rivals are without a doubt going to be your leave procedure assuming that circumstances become difficult. If you exist in a current bubble and then things tighten up across your industry, consolidation can be a good way to upsize a business quickly or improve a business that is drowning on its own.

If they trust you, they will be much more happy with getting you. Assuming they know you, and they address you frequently and you have shown that you have them covered, they will be much more open to a consolidation conversation instead of in the event that you just rang them in the hotness of desperation.

Mergers are an extraordinary approach to level up your business and bring more noteworthy capability and assets into an association. At the point when two associations become one, there is normally the worth which brings about two tasks meeting up, sharing what works and what doesn't work. There is efficiencies acquired through the combination of assets and there is strength bringing about the united market share.

So call your rivals and say Hi, present yourself and stay in contact. You simply never know when you will require them.

Rule 16 - Know your numbers, all of them.

"Realize your numbers' is a principal statute of business." - Bill Gates

It is an essential rule for any great director isn't it, know your numbers. If you can't read a profit and loss statement, or a cash flow statement then make sure you can before you launch your new enterprise.

What numbers do you truly have to zero in on the most when you are sending off your new pursuit? Every one of them, one of the main weapons in your munititions stockpile is your information, on the off chance that you don't approach information your dead in the water. Whenever you are building your business, prior to sending off your very interesting item or administration set up cycles and innovation to guarantee you catch all information any place possible.

A decent bookkeeping programming bundle will give you all that you really want to be aware of income, financial plan versus genuine, benefit and misfortune and an accounting report. You want however to get significantly more complex than that. Before you start, track down a strategy for catching client data and purchasing conduct, it is the best technique for profoundly getting what accomplishes and doesn't work in your business.

By understanding your client's purchasing conduct, you can make sense of your own client patterns. Who your clients are, how old they are, the place where do they reside, when do they purchase? This sort of data is urgent in the improvement of compelling promoting strategies.

They say that 80% of your organizations come from 20% of your clients. By having great strong information on your clients and their purchasing conduct you can remunerate steadfast clients with limits, select offers and rewards.

By understanding what they purchase and when, you can foster client explicit advertising programs that elevate items and administrations to your clients that you definitely realize they are keen on. Greeting just offers that are designated in view of their very own advantages and past purchasing conduct is the most impressive promoting instrument you might at any point roll out.

Comprehensively understanding your numbers will drive your business technique and probable outcome in the plan and execution of capacities or client benefits that will essentially assist you with accomplishing significantly more deals. Amazon.com do it very well on the web, that basic calculation that they have fostered that shows up upon the checkout, 'individuals who purchased the item you're purchasing likewise purchased this item'. That one little gadget on

their checkout has driven deals through the rooftop as they are plainly showing the client items they are reasonable intrigued in.

Rule 17 – Be humble.

"Lowliness isn't considering less yourself, its reasoning of yourself less." - *Rick Warren*

Are you looking for notoriety and fortune? Extravagant your face on the front of fortune 500 magazine? Need to one day come to the rich 200 rundown? That is so cool. I genuinely trust you get that sort of progress. Let the world put you there and don't tragically attempt to persuade individuals that you're well en route to that sort of notoriety.

If you are laying out another business, don't wrongly allow your self image to pull off you. Sure you are presently an individual from a little modest bunch of individuals on the planet who have the balls to go solo and have a go. You are a daring person, you are a business visionary. I don't have any idea how frequently I have sat with individuals and stood by listening to them go wild on about how effective the organization will be, the means by which they have an edge on the lookout, this is all there is to it, the start of their empire.

By acting this way you split apart you and everybody around you, assuming your business bombs every individual who heard you going on and on over on about how extraordinary you are and the way that amazing your business will be, later groaned to their spouses returning about how you wouldn't quiet down. Assuming your business goes under they will savor your disappointment.

Be unassuming; don't allow your inner self to get the better of you. Take individuals on the excursion with you, and recollect whether your business bombs your companions are without a doubt going to help you out in your season of need.

Rule 18 - If your robbing Peter to Pay Paul, downsize immediately

"Money is the craft of passing cash from one hand to another until it at last vanishes." - Robert W. Sarnoff

Having some cash flow issues? Company is a bit short of money but you expect things will pick up again? Sales have become a bit seasonal? Just a slow period at the moment but it will turn around? Is your cash flow management a daily program? What has hit the account today? Let's just pay the creditors who are screaming the loudest and we will clear the back log of debt when things pick up again. Think about what, you are presently exchanging insolvent.

If you wind up taking from one to give to another you really want to quickly act. Before long as this happens start a drive of cost removing straight. Got a more clean? Dispose of them! Do you have water being conveyed for the staff? Allow them to drink faucet water! Got two or three staff cruising along agreeable in their jobs, dispose of one of them. Give your best for lessen your expenses any place you can, slice and consume anything across the association that is consuming money. You are obviously better to put increment strain on an association for a period than continue to exchange yourself into an opening that you can't get out of.

You should constantly run after being income positive; it is a receptive cycle that you truly need to continuously have an idea about. Aspect your association to the levels it can stand to keep up with, in the event that incomes go up, increment your association to additionally foster development, assuming incomes go down, scale back your association likewise. Work a powerful association; it is the best way to endure the highs and lows that happen while carrying on with work in any market. Ultimately, never exchange ruined, on the off chance that it appears as though you can't cut back the business to a point that it can in any case work, close up shop right away. Keep in mind, the life span of your business isn't simply determined by your portion of the overall industry yet your capacity to rapidly adjust to your outer and inward realities.

Rule 19 – Never bring your misery to the workplace.

"I discovered that mental fortitude was not the shortfall of dread, but rather the victory over it. The daring man would he say he is who doesn't feel apprehensive, yet he who vanquishes fear."
- Nelson Mandela

Are you drained, broken down? Tired of the drudgery? Been working 15 hours every day for the last month in your new pursuit and presently you're over it? Well anything that you really do don't impart your wretchedness to your representatives, providers or clients. As the head of your association you set the way of life, in the event that you are consistently groaning about the difficulties the business is confronting you will obliterate your corporate culture. Get a coach, converse with your significant other and family and guarantee you show energy, excitement and strength in the work place. Your representatives are taking a gander at you for authority and bearing, don't let them somewhere near showing them that you're human, particularly when you are confronting a few difficulties inside your business.

Nobody needs to work for a blithering, crushed hopeless has been. So strengthen, drink yourself a jar of solidify up and continue ahead with it. If you are wallowing in self-pity and helplessness then you have some serious commercial issue that you need to address, or if you are having some domestic issues at home make sure you park them at the door of your workplace. You set the way of life at your work spot, and hopelessness is contagious.

Be unequivocal; contact other effective individuals outside of your work place for exhortation or conference. Continuously keep up with the façade of being in charge, regardless of whether the dividers are tumbling down around you. On the off chance that you flounder your workers will call it quits when you want them the most. Try not to let business issues putrefy, don't get self-satisfied and embrace the view that issues will simply figure out themselves, they will not. You and you alone can resolve them so get into stuff and begin resolving the issues individually, make an individual activity plan and get to work.

Rule 20 - Don't betray your values to make a buck, it will destroy your soul.

"The board is doing things right; administration is doing the right things." - *Peter Drucker*

As my last example in this book, I have left it last as I really do trust it to be the most important illustration of all. The issue with values is at times you don't realize you even have them until you have double-crossed them. Yet, more often than not we know what we are open to doing and what we are not happy doing. The vast majority of us have an enthusiasm for our ethical compass and what lines we in all likelihood will not cross.

Being in your own business especially during the foundation stage can make lines of pressure between your qualities and what requirements to end up pushing the business ahead. Assuming that you're a representative, you might wind up being approached to accomplish something you're not happy with and you might decline, as an entrepreneur you might end up with the decision of deceiving your qualities to keep the business alive.

Sometimes we make splits the difference with ourselves and our qualities, in circumstances where decisions should be made, hard decisions, we frequently end up with the quandary of asking ourselves which values am I more open to selling out than others? You're likely perusing this presently thinking, what is he happening about? I will not sell out my qualities, of all time. You will however end up in the middle of the pressure of individual qualities and business, and how you answer could mean the continuation or the finish of your enterprise.

Faced with this choice, how might you respond? Double-cross your qualities and push the business ahead? All things considered, you want the business for money, your life reserve funds are enveloped with it. Or on the other hand do you not double-cross your qualities and lose the lot?

Well, I once permitted myself to be tormented into double-crossing my qualities. As a minority investor in an organization I was running, I was frequently tormented into going with choices that conflicted with my very own qualities. The business result was incredible, incomes were up, and staff kept their positions and my different investors as partners were fulfilled that I was doing everything humanly conceivable to accomplish a positive business result. The issue was I wasn't content with myself at all, and understandably. Without a doubt, what I was approached to do had a huge momentary enhancement for income, yet the consequences of the choice wound up costing the organization huge sums in lawful charges and brand damage.

The result not just financially affected the business, it appallingly affected me by and by. It simply wasn't what My identity was, I don't go around doing things like that, I'm not wired that way, and I deceived my very own values.

If you wind up at a go across streets where you really want to act against your very own qualities, track down an alternate arrangement, or quit. Try not to permit anyone to menace you or at any point let anyone drive you to accomplish something you might regularly want to do. Each time you deceive your own qualities it resembles ingesting poison, a smidgen at a time.

Don't at any point think twice about values to earn anything, it will decimate you. I solidly accept that strong, rich men without any compunctions have destroyed their worth framework individually, gradually selling out them and disposing of them until there aren't any qualities left whatsoever. These influential individuals will more often than not become increasingly more remarkable as they consume the kindness of kind individuals with great intentions.

Stay consistent with yourself, get your qualities and make those esteems the upsides of your organization. Get everyone from financial backers to representatives to focus on maintaining those qualities, as Google vows to do no shrewd, what values will you and your kin maintain in your organization? I wish you all the outcome in your business, be strong, persist or more all be consistent with yourself.